Contents:

The blue pages

On the blue pages you will find general information relevant to the aquarium hobby. If you already have fishkeeping experience you can skip them.

But we have chosen this method because we have no idea what you already know, and constant references to other literature are not much help.

How the guppy got its name

Nowadays every child knows the guppy, but it was not always so. The destinies of the guppy and humans first began to intertwine about 140 years ago. In 1856 the first preserved specimen from Venezuela reached the huge collection in the Berlin Museum. It originated from a river in that country, the Guayre, close to the large coastal city of Caracas. The ichthyologist PETERS, who was working at the Berlin Museum at the time, identified 1859 the little fish as a scientifically unknown species and described it as *Poecilia reticulata*. Peters didn't give it a common name.

The genus *Poecilia* had been erected 58 years earlier, likewise by scientists working in Berlin, namely BLOCH & SCHNEIDER. The name derives from the Greek word poikilos, which has numerous meanings on a theme of "varied" including "variegated", which is perhaps what they had in mind. Hence *Poecilia* can be translated as "variegated fish". The type species of the genus is *Poecilia vivipara*, which is now only rarely maintained in the aquarium. The word vivipara means "livebearing".

Thus Peters named his fish – and the Latin is highly appropriate – "variegated fish with a net-like pattern", as reticulata means "reticulated". But Peters in fact had no idea how colorful the guppy is. How so? Quite simply, Peters' specimen was a female, and so he likewise can have had no idea that he had discovered what was subsequently to become one of the most popular fish species in the world on account of its splendid coloration.

The fact that males were initially unknown also explains why Peters' colleague GÜNTHER, working at the Natural History Museum in London, in 1866 described the species again as apparently new. He had specimens from Venezuela and Trinidad. He named the species

Poecilia vivipara, the One spot molly

Girardinus guppii in honor of the collector who had sent him the fishes – the Reverend Guppy, a priest working in Trinidad, or so the story goes.

The first live guppies reached Germany from Venezuela in 1908, and were correctly identified as *Poecilia reticulata*. But later on specimens also arrived from Trinidad and were identified as *Girardinus guppii* as they differed in color from the specimens already known. There followed a major dispute over the correct name of these fishes, the more so as additional stocks arrived from Barbados, from where the Italian scholar DE FILIPPI had described the species *Lebistes poecilioides* in 1861. In fact – as revealed by a little detective work by Fred POESER and Isaäc ISBRÜCKER in 2002 – they were not guppies at all, and not even from Barbados, but probably a *Limia* species from Jamaica. The outcome of all the argument was the realization that all three species were the same – and the name "guppy".

The scientific species name

The scientific classification of the animal and plant kingdoms requires a unified system of nomenclature. Obviously animals and plants also have common names in their natural distribution areas, but these names are not governed by any rules, and so widespread species also have numerous popular names. Take the plant shown here. It grows all over Europe, and I first encountered it as rabbit food! The English call it dandelion, a corruption of the French dent de lion, and in Germany it is Löwenzahn, in both cases meaning "lion's tooth", referring to the jagged-edged leaves. But the French also call it pis-en-lit, referring to its diuretic properties, and the Germans have a host of other names: Milchbusch (milk bush), from the milky sap that oozes from broken stems; Pusteblume (blow-flower), from the fluffy ripe seed-heads which it is such fun to blow away; and Butterblume (butter flower), a collective name for yellow-flowered plants of summer meadows. All these names for one species, and I am sure there must be more.

It was obvious that the scientific classification of the animal and plant species of the world required a system that would permit understanding regardless of geographical boundaries. Such a system was devised by the Swedish biologist CARL VON LINNÉ (who, following the fashion of his time, preferred the Latinized version of his name, CAROLUS LINNAEUS). His basic idea was as simple as it was ingenious. First, he decreed, to be internationally valid names must be given in a dead language, as only names with no national connotations would gain international acceptance. In addition, these names must consist of two parts. This system had already been tried and tested in the naming of humans, where each person has a personal and a family name. Linné therefore decided that closely related species should be grouped together in genera. Thus each species has a genus name followed by a species name. The genus name begins with an upper case (capital) letter, the species name with a lower case one. In addition, the name of the describer follows the species name, followed by a comma and the year of the original description. This makes it possible to locate the work in which the species was described. Thus the plant shown here is scientifically known as *Taraxacum officinale* LINNÉ, 1758.

As already mentioned, the first live guppies reached Europe - more precisely, England - back in 1906. The first importations into Germany took place in December 1908, from Venezuela (as *Poecilia reticulata*), and more guppies were imported in 1909 from Trinidad (as *Girardinus guppii*) and Barbados (as *Poecilia poecilioides*).

These first specimens were very expensive, as can be seen from the advertisement to the right. Very few hobbyists could afford 2 to 5 marks per pair. The later imports were even more expensive, with a pair of *Girardinus guppii* costing as much as 80 marks. Although it is, of course, very difficult to convert such sums to current values, as a rough guide, one gold mark is about the equivalent of 10 US dollars. But in those days it was common for the aquarium and terrarium clubs by then in existence to pool their resources to buy a box of livestock, with the animals then given to selected members to breed. As guppies proved easy to breed, the price fell very rapidly.

Before long guppies became the desirable exotic species that even beginners could afford. Once it became known that all three forms were just a single species, there was no further concern about maintaining pure bloodlines. Guppies, already highly variable in the wild, were rendered more attractive, and their finnage even more variable, by the crossing of local forms. By as early as 1910 there were reports of guppies with greatly enlarged dorsal and caudal fins, and more prominent "swords" in the lower caudal. By 1918 most of the tail forms we see today were already known, or at least being developed. Golden guppies appeared in 1933-34. The delta tail so popular today has been known since the 1950s.

Nowadays the main centers of guppy breeding are in Singapore, Hongkong, Sri Lanka, Israel, and Florida. Almost

Vereinigte Zierfischzüchtereien in Conradshöhe b. Tegel.

CONRADSHÖHE

Poecilia reticulata Peters
mit einigen in Farben und Schwanzflossen verschiedenen Männchen.
=== Die Männchen dieser Art sind durchweg in Farben variierend. ===
Preis per Paar **2** bis **5** Mark.
Ferner offerieren wir:
Rasbora heteromorpha, Rasbora cephalotaenia, Rasbora maculata, Rasbora elegans, Barbus fasciolatus, Acantophthalmus Kuhlii, Callichthys marmoratus, Monopterus javanensis, Plecostomus Commersoni, Xenomystus nigri.

This advert appeared in 1910 in the magazine *Wochenschrift für Aquarien- und Terrarienkunde*. The picture of guppies is by A. SCHLAWINSKI (1909).

all the guppies sold in the trade come from professional fish-breeding farms in these areas. On the hobby front, guppy societies in various countries, especially the USA, England, Holland, Germany, and Japan, are actively involved in the further line-breeding of these little jewels.

After our short historical review, it is now time to turn to the present. What sort of aquarium should we set up in which to keep and breed guppies? Regardless of the size of the container, it is a fact that guppies are very sensitive to bacterial pollution of the water. The alpha and omega of guppy care are thus an aquarium that has been properly matured biologically and one that is carefully maintained. As regards aquarium size (please also see the general page, "How large an aquarium?"), for a small group of 3-4 males and 2-3 females an aquarium 40 x 20 x 20 cm (tank sizes are always given length x width x height) will suffice. But in that case no additional fishes should be introduced to the tank.

This very beautiful guppy aquarium is planted with *Cabomba* and water wistaria (*Hygrophila difformis*).

rature in the guppy aquarium should never drop below about 30°C for long. The ideal temperature is 24-26°C, the upper limit about 30°C. Both upper and lower temperature limits should be approached very gradually. Modern aquarium heating equipment is almost invariably thermostatically controlled and keeps the water temperature stable within a 1°C range. Very many German guppy keepers have achieved good results by turning the heating off with the lights when the aquarium is sited in a room where normal room temperature is maintained night and day. This will result in the water temperature dropping by a few degrees C overnight, and then rising again by day to the thermostatically controlled level of, for example, 25°C. These relatively small fluctuations in the day-night rhythm have a very positive effect on the immune response of guppies - they become livelier and less susceptible to disease.

An aquarium of, for example, 60 x 30 x 30 cm is better, and nowadays it is often possible to buy a reasonably-priced complete "set-up", consisting of tank, filter, heating, and lighting. Such an aquarium can house about 15 adult guppies.

Guppies are tropical fishes, hence the water tempe-

Guppy aquaria should be well lit, as guppies depend on visual stimuli. At the same time, good illumination is a prerequisite for good aquatic plant growth. Because guppies are very lively fishes, they have a high metabolic rate. Vigorous plant growth is generally capable of reducing some metabolic poisons to harmless concentrations. More on this in the chapter "Plants in the Guppy Aquarium". Nowadays the aquarium is almost invariably lit by means of fluorescent tubes. The number of tubes required will depend primarily on the depth of water. The tubes should always be as long as the tank so there are no dark corners. For water depths of 20-30 cm one tube per 30 cm of aquarium width will suffice. A couple of examples: aquarium 100 x 30 x 30 cm, one tube; aquarium 100 x 40 x 30 cm, two tubes. For 40-50 cm of water depth, two tubes per 30 cm of tank width are required to ensure good plant growth. For tanks 60 cm or more deep, it may be better to install HQI lamps.

If, for whatever reason, only a single internal power filter is to be used, then abundant plant growth is essential. It is better to use external canister in conjunction with a UV sterilizer. As a general rule of thumb, the nominal hourly turnover rate of such filters should be about double the gross water capacity of the aquarium, ie 120 liters per hour for a 60 liter aquarium.

Important: filters should never be switched off along with the lighting and (if relevant) heating. The filter is required at night as well, in order to suppress a rise in the carbon dioxide level resulting from the respiration of the plants. Moreover, if the filter is turned off, the useful filter bacteria will die off,

Detail of the aquarium shown on the previous page. Provided guppies are not alarmed, they will by preference remain in open water and not hide among the plants.

possibly resulting in lethal ammonia and nitrite poisoning in the fishes.

When it comes to the aquarium decor, the imagination of the aquarist can be given virtually a free rein. However, rocks should never be sharp-edged, to avoid injury to the fishes. Moreover, rocks should never - and this applies to the aquarium hobby in general - contain metallic inclusions. All the types of wood typically in use in the hobby can be included in the guppy aquarium. Wood should, however, be soaked for at least two weeks before aquarium use, and the water in the soaking container changed as often as possible. This will leach out the harmless substances in the wood that would otherwise seriously diminish the transparency of the aquarium water. After soaking the wood should be scrubbed clean under a running tap using a coarse brush, and then it can be placed in the aquarium.

The substrate also plays an important role in the guppy aquarium. The top layer should, wherever possible, consist of fine sand. Guppies prefer to feed on small morsels of food, and if the substrate is too coarse then may food particles may fall down between the grains where the fishes cannot reach it. The result is unnecessary pollution of the aquarium by the metabolic products of the bacteria that cause putrefaction. On the one hand this may lead to sickness in the guppies, on the other it may encourage undesirable, rampant algal growth. In particular the dreaded and difficult to combat "blue-green algae" (Cyanobacte-

ria), which manifest as a dark blue-green, slimy film over plants, hard decor, and equipment, and choke all the life beneath, may proliferate rapidly in such circumstances.

When setting up your guppy aquarium, please make sure that you do not include too many items of decor. On the one hand these will limit swimming space unnecessarily, while on the other they will significantly reduce the net volume of water.

This aquarium is well suited to keeping guppies, although a top layer of fine sand on the bottom would be beneficial.

How large an aquarium

In aquarium circles there is a saying, "An aquarium can never be too large." How so? Well, the main reason is that the body of water in the aquarium is more stable, chemically speaking, the larger its volume. In other words, a large aquarium is significantly less work than a small one.

Beginners and non-aquarists often think that fishes feel like prisoners in a small aquarium. This is not the case. Compared with the wild, even a large aquarium is no more than a tiny puddle, but fishes have no more concept of freedom than do other animals - such an abstraction is of no biological relevance to them. Only mankind has an inbred desire for freedom, and even so the concept has no single definition. Just ask 10 people of your acquaintance, what they understand by "freedom". In all probability you will get 10 different answers. In actuality, Man's quest for freedom is the recipe for his evolutionary success. It is nothing more than an innate feeling of discontent with the individual's personal circumstances, in consequence of which, depending on the degree of dissatisfaction, the person concerned seeks for an opportunity to alter his or her situation. By virtue of his inventive genius Man can adapt his environment to his needs and hence survive literally anywhere. In short, the human quest for freedom is a natural species-specific survival factor.

By contrast animals, including all fishes, are incapable of adapting their environment to their needs. Instead they are dependent, for better or worse, on their ability to adapt to their present environmental conditions. A blenny that decided to abandon its troglodytic existence for the lifestyle of a herring would survive only a few hours. Thus animals have no freedom. And thus the question of how large an aquarium has nothing to do with the amount of space available to a fish in nature. The aquarist should instead ask, "Would the fish species that I want to keep colonize my aquarium if the habitat it provides occurred in the wild?"

The significant differences between an optimal aquarium and the wild are: there are no enemies; there is an unlimited food supply; there is no competition; there are no natural catastrophes (drought, flood, etc) - the aquarist ensures all these things.

Accordingly the tank size necessary is a function of the expected eventual size and the behavior of the fishes. For inactive predators, that spend the entire day lying motionless in wait for prey, the tank length should be about three times, the tank width about twice, the body length of the fish. For active shoaling fishes the rule of thumb is a tank length at least 10 times body length, and tank width five times. Finally, the number of fishes must be taken into account. And here the old aquarists rule remains valid - at least two liters of water per cm of fish length.

If you are thinking of setting up an aquarium, please always bear its maintenance requirements in mind. Every aquarium requires a weekly or fortnightly partial water change of 10-25% of its volume. This removes pollutants, the accumulated waste products from metabolic processes, and also replaces depleted trace elements. For a 1000 liter aquarium that means 200-500 liters of water to be shifted (100-250 liters out, and the same back in). As a new recruit to the hobby you will do best to start with an aquarium of 150-300 liters capacity. A tank of this size will provide a chemically very stable volume of water and is a good size for almost all the aquarium fishes normally available in the trade.

Chemistry – how water works

Even if you have previously regarded chemistry as not your particular cup of tea, a few basic elements of chemical knowledge will not come amiss in the aquarist.

First of all there is water hardness. Most people will already have heard of this, as water hardness is responsible for the "chalking up" of kettles, hot water pipes, etc. The concept of water hardness originates from the washing powder industry and was originally used to quantify the amount of soap powder needed to create an effective lather for washing. Only later was it discovered that it was calcium and magnesium compounds dissolved in the water that were responsible for the greater or lesser soap requirement. The terms "hard" and "soft" derive from the sensation evoked by soap lather on the skin in the water in question.

From an aquarium viewpoint it is mainly the so-called "carbonate hardness" (KH, expressed in degrees) that is important. It is a measure of the compounds calcium and magnesium carbonate, which react with carbonic acid to form calcium and magnesium bicarbonate. Because they are chemically unstable, both these substances play an important role in the aquarium. They react reciprocally with carbonic acid and can be problematical per se for so-called "softwater fishes" that practically never encounter them in nature. In addition there are yet other calcium and magnesium compounds in water, which, however, are relatively stable chemically and of no great practical significance. These are designated "non-carbonate hardness". The two forms of hardness combined make up general hardness (GH), also measured in degrees, which in this case vary from country to country - those used in this book are German, °dGH. 0-4 °dGH denotes (roughly) very soft, 4-8 °dGH soft, 8-12 °dGH medium hard, 12-18 °dGH hard, 18-30 °dGH very hard, and more than 30 °dGH extremely hard, water.

The pH value is closely connected with hardness, although they are totally separate concepts chemically. The pH value denotes the degree of acidity of the water. It is important to realize that pH is measured using a logarithmic decimal scale, so that water with a pH of 5 is 10 times as acid as pH 6, and 100 times as acid as pH 7. Because the components of carbonate hardness react very strongly with acids, in the aquarium mainly with carbonic acid, the concepts of hardness and pH are very much intertwined from an aquarium viewpoint. Water with a pH of 7 is designated neutral, water with a ph above 7 is termed alkaline, and that with a pH below 7 is acid. The extremes that (specialized) fishes can tolerate are an acid pH of 3.5 and an alkaline pH of 9.5.

The pH can fluctuate dramatically with the day-night rhythm, and this is often the reason why fishes become sick or die. The reason for this pH fluctuation is that at night plants do not use carbon dioxide as they are not engaged in photosynthesis, and in fact actually give off additional carbon dioxide via their respiration. In hard water this has little effect, as the carbonate hardness "cancels out" the carbon dioxide (the technical term for this is "buffering"). However, soft water has little or no buffering capacity (i.e. carbonate hardness) and this can result in pH surges that are life-threatening for the fishes.

There are three methods of avoiding this danger. Firstly an airstone can be used in the aquarium at night. Carbon dioxide is highly volatile and can thus easily be driven off from the water. Alternatively, humic acid can be added via peat filtration or as a liquid preparation, and this will also have a buffering effect, though this method can be used only for fishes that will tolerate acid water. Otherwise, for fish that don't like acidity, the water must be artificially hardened - method 3.

Hardness and pH should be monitored regularly.

Plants perform a number of functions in the guppy aquarium. They remove pollutants, which serve them as food for growth. They provide hiding places for harassed adults and newborn fry. They produce oxygen and reduce carbon dioxide levels during the day. And finally, a planted aquarium is much more attractive than a bare tank.

It is best to choose problem-free, fast-growing plants for the guppy aquarium, as these will best perform the functions required of them. Choice of the correct substrate is important for a planted aquarium - it must be at least 7 cm, better 10 cm, deep. At the bottom you can use a layer of "compost" material containing a long-term mineral fertilizer in the form of special clay or similar. Horticultural fertilizers and composts are totally unsuitable as these have a high content of organic nutrients that will pollute the aquarium and ruin the water quality. On top of the compost there should be a 5-7 cm layer of fine aquarium gravel, which should, as usual, be thoroughly washed before use. Finally there is the top layer, and

in the case of the guppy aquarium this should be a 2 cm layer of fine sand, again painstakingly washed clean.

Next carefully add just enough water to thoroughly moisten the substrate. This will enable you to plant the aquarium without a load of "dirt" floating up from the bottom layers. Once all the plants are in position, you can - carefully! - fill the aquarium with pre-warmed (to 19-22°C) water. Finally set the filtration and heating going. Now the aquarium should remain unoccupied for at least two weeks - this is necessary to allow the aquarium to develop the population of microorganisms needed to turn a sterile tank of water into a functional aquarium biotope. During this period the plants will start to grow and so the lighting must be turned on right away.

Attractively planted aquaria are decorative and a healthy environment for guppies.

"Vallis", *Vallisneria* **spp.**

Vallis (scientific name *Vallisneria*) species are all eminently suited to the guppy aquarium. They are very rapid-growing, rosette-forming plants, that reproduce abundantly via runners. There are a number of species, the majority difficult to tell apart. *Vallisneria* such as those pictured above should be sited at the rear of the aquarium where they will soon form a dense jungle of leaves 40-60 cm long. Two *Vallisneria* species deserve special mention. The first is corkscrew vallis (*Vallisneria americana* var. *biwaensis*); it

generally grows to only about 20 cm tall and is thus a prime candidate for small aquaria. The other is giant vallis (*Vallisneria americana* var. *americana*), whose up to 3 cm wide leaves can attain a length of up to 150 cm - hence this plant should be grown only in large aquaria.

Vallisneria generally prefer medium-hard water, but will grow satisfactorily in almost all conditions. There are both male and female plants. The flowers are very insignificant.

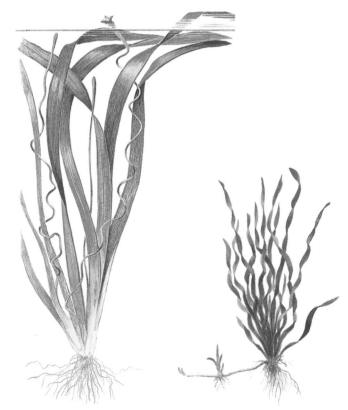

Giant vallis   Corkscrew vallis

Small-leaved willowleaf

Small-leaved willowleaf, pink-veined cultivated form

Water wistaria

Small-leaved willowleaf (*Hygrophila polysperma*) and water wistaria (*H. difformis*)

Small-leaved willowleaf and water wistaria are stemmed plants and can be planted in clumps in the guppy aquarium. If they are regularly "stopped" then they will form decorative bushy growth, but if allowed to grow freely they will extend along the surface and send attractive adventitious roots down into the water. This type of growth creates excellent cover for guppy fry. Both species are also available in colorful cultivated forms - the pink-veined form of the willowleaf is shown above right.

Amazon swordplants (*Echinodorus bleheri*)

Many species of the genus *Echinodorus* are cultivated in aquaria, all of them attractive and desirable. However, that pictured above is particularly suited to the guppy aquarium on account of its rapid growth and undemanding nature. Depending on light and water conditions, it grows to between 20 and 50 cm tall. It is a rosette-forming plant that soon forms a stout bush creating a highly decorative effect. It adapts well to a variety of water conditions, for which reason it is recommended here. At the same time it is a good bio-indicator of iron deficiency in the aquarium - if the new foliage is yellow and brittle, the cause is almost always an iron and/or manganese deficiency. These two trace elements work together reciprocally. Special fertilizers can be purchased. Propagation is via plantlets that form on the flowering stems if these are kept below water. These can be detached and planted once they have formed 5-7 leaves.

Indian fern

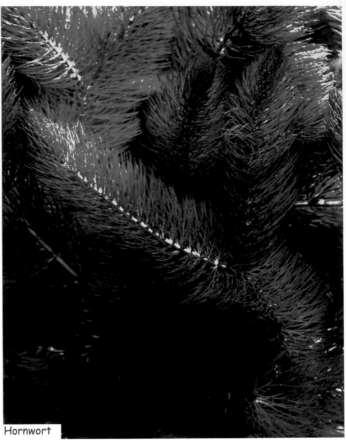
Hornwort

Indian or Sumatra fern (*Ceratopteris thalictroides*)

Indian (or Sumatra) fern is a rosette-forming plant that can be grown rooted or floating. In the latter case it is an excellent refuge for fry. Abundant plantlets form in the leaf axils. This plant adapts splendidly to all water conditions and grows very rapidly.

Hornwort (*Ceratophyllum demersum*)

Hornwort is a stemmed plant that never forms roots, hence it can be grown loose in the water. It will, however, also tolerate being pushed into the substrate. Hornwort is very useful in the breeding aquarium and provides outstanding shelter for fry.

There are, of course, many more plants suitable for the guppy aquarium. Those covered here will, however, thrive even if the aquarist doesn't have a "green thumb", and hence can be unreservedly recommended.

Planting plants

Basically, three types of plants are cultivated in the aquarium: floating plants, stemmed, and rosette-forming plants.

The floating plants are most easily "planted". They are simply placed on the water's surface, and all that is necessary is to make sure the roots are pointing downwards - and even that is superfluous with the rootless types. All floating plants "dislike" filter currents, and it is often pointless to try and grow them in heavily filtered aquaria.

Stemmed plants form only a moderately extensive root structure. They are propagated via cuttings taken from any stems that are long enough. As a rule cuttings should be about 10 cm long. When planting stemmed plants the following points should be noted: never plant them in bundles, but insert each stem separately. The lower leaves should be removed, as if buried in the substrate they will rot and possibly infect the stem with decay. When you buy stemmed plants from an aquarium store, they will usually be clipped together with lead or planted in a small pot - the lead or pot should be removed before planting. Finally, remove any roots already present. If the lower stem looks transparent then it has been squashed - cut off the affected part with a sharp knife before planting the remainder.

Finally, the third group of plants comprises the rosette-forming types. These plants form an extensive root structure. They are propagated via runners or offsets. With these plants too, any lead strip or pot must be removed before planting, and the roots should then be gently teased out and shortened to about 3 cm long using a sharp knife. When planting, it is essential that the roots all point downwards into the planting hole - if they get bent upwards during planting then the plant will not grow well. Rosette-forming plants possess a "crown" or woody rootstock (rhizome) from which the foliage grows, and it is important to ensure that this growing point is not buried in the substrate but extends a few millimeters above it.

A number of rosette-forming plants of the genus *Anubias*, as well as ferns of the genera *Microsorium* and *Bolbitis*, do not grow well if planted in the substrate. These plants are best tied to wood or porous stones using dark cotton, and will attach themselves firmly in time. These plants can often be purchased growing on rocks or wood.

Many rosette-forming plants are marsh plants by nature, and grow submerged only part of the time in their natural habitat. To this group belong many species of the genera *Cryptocoryne* and *Echinodorus*, for example. When first planting an aquarium, these plants should generally make up only about a third of the species used. This is because these plants grow only relatively slowly. During the initial phase of a new aquarium the biological conditions are such that many undesirable algae find an optimal environment for growth. Because aquatic plants and algae compete with one another for resources, logically fast-growing plants will be more successful than slow-growing ones. Your dealer will, of course, be pleased to advise which plants will be suited to your aquarium. But if you want an extensive discussion with your dealer it is best not to visit him during his busy period - this also applies when the object is to design a planting scheme.

Biological equilibrium in the aquarium

It is impossible to achieve a true biological equilibrium in the aquarium - that must be understood right from the start. The amount of extraneous nutrients (in the form of fish food) is simply too great. One can - and should - nevertheless endeavor to create a stable aquarium environment which must then be supported by partial water changes and filter cleaning.

The basic prerequisite for such a stable aquarium environment is the use of water of consistent initial quality. That is to say, that the water used for changes should be identical in hardness and pH with that already in the aquarium. So think this over carefully before deciding on "home-brewed" water instead of your mains water. Because you will have to prepare it yourself, week-in, week-out!

The aquarium hobby is essentially about culturing bacteria. Without these invisible helpers it is impossible to run an aquarium. On the one hand there are the nitrite-forming bacteria. Fishes constantly excrete highly toxic ammonia (from the breakdown of protein) from their gills, and this first group of essential helpful bacteria convert this ammonia into nitrite (still highly toxic, and normally lethal to fishes in concentrations of 1 mg/liter). The bacteria need oxygen to convert ammonia to nitrite, and hence are termed aerobic bacteria. The second group of bacteria that make it possible for fish to live in aquaria are also aerobic, and convert the still highly toxic nitrite into relatively harmless nitrate. When maintaining an aquarium the aim should be a nitrate level of about 30 mg/liter; the value should never be appreciably higher, but lower is OK.

It is always the same genera of bacteria that perform this important nitrification, but every aquarium will have its own "micro-climate" depending on its basic water parameters, i.e. hardness and pH. The bacteria are appreciably more sensitive than fishes to fluctuations in water parameters, hence it is immensely important always to use "matching" water for water changes.

As well as the aerobic nitrifying bacteria there are innumerable other micro-organisms, i.e. bacteria, fungi, etc, that colonize aquaria. The higher the nutrient loading of the aquarium, the higher the number of these organisms in the water. Additional factors that increase the micro-organism population include the fish population density and the amount of convertible organic material in the aquarium, i.e. the so-called mulm. Mulm consists of fish excreta, dead vegetation, uneaten food, etc, and it makes no difference whether it is lying around the tank or out of sight in the filter! The organisms that process mulm are intrinsically harmless, but if their population increases to excess then these normally harmless organisms represent a danger to the fishes. The immune systems of many fishes kept in aquaria are naturally only weakly developed, as the micro-organism population in many tropical waters is extremely low because they are very nutrient-poor. Hence it is obvious that the micro-organism population should be kept as low as possible by siphoning off mulm during water changes, filter maintenance, and sensible limitation of the fish population.

Should it be necessary, for whatever reason, to populate the aquarium densely with fishes, then a UV sterilizer, installed in the filter return, is one way of effectively reducing the number of micro-organisms in the water. But – and this is where skill comes in – the aquarist should always seek to create a degree of biological equilibrium through knowledge and thought, and use special equipment only where unavoidable.

How a filter works

There are many different types of filter, all with advantages and disadvantages. Basically, every filter has a mechanical and a biological section. The former serves to remove particles – that cloud the water or are regarded as dirt - from the aquarium. For this purpose the aquarium water is drawn through a suitable filter medium and the cleansed water is then pumped back into the aquarium. This mechanical cleansing is usually achieved using filter floss, sponge, or the like. You should get into the habit of cleaning this "dirt filter" weekly during the partial water change. Ideally the filter medium should be rinsed in a bucket of newly siphoned-off the aquarium water, as this will avoid harm to the useful aerobic bacteria also contained in the medium.

The biological section is usually divided into various zones. The best-known is the aerobic zone, which endeavors to produce the largest possible population of the aerobic bacteria that convert ammonia to nitrate via nitrite, by providing a substrate with the largest possible surface area for colonization. This process is strictly oxygen-dependent. Typical substrates include ceramic tubes, "bioballs", various artificial materials, porous clay balls, and even basalt chips. The most extreme form of the aerobic filter is the so-called trickle filter, in which the water cascades over thin layers of filter media and is thus constantly supplied with abundant oxygen. This works exceptionally well, although only miserable plant growth is possible when the water is processed this way, and in addition the high oxygen level encourages rampant algal growth. For this reason such filters are best used only for heavily populated aquaria with alkaline water, where the danger of ammonia toxicity is greatest.

More and more frequently the aerobic filter indispensable in any aquarium is nowadays complemented by an anaerobic filter, inhabited by anaerobic bacteria to which oxygen is toxic.

These filters have two great advantages. Firstly they can be used to cultivate bacteria that break down the relatively harmless nitrate into gaseous nitrogen and oxygen. Both gases can then escape from the water. If the filter functions properly then it can thus be used to keep the level of nitrate in the aquarium very low. Secondly, in this type of filter the highly important plant nutrients that are oxidized by aerobic filters (and thus rendered useless to plants) undergo reduction, i.e. the oxygen is removed again. For this reason many aquarists run a slow-flow anaerobic filter in bypass, i.e. connected to the outlet of the aerobic filter.

There are various media for anaerobic filters. Special artificial media are used for the nitrate reduction filter, sold already impregnated with the required bacterial culture. As a rule a small external filter with a low throughput is used for the plant-friendly bypass filter, and filled with, for example, fine sand or special filter media such as sintered glass, etc. Your dealer will be pleased to advise on this.

The filter can also contain materials with a special purpose, for example filter carbon. This so-called activated carbon is very effective for removing some medication residues from the water, as well as yellowing and other types of discoloration. Filter carbon should be used only for a specific purpose, not on a permanent basis. In addition a bag of peat can be placed in the filter to acidify the water. There are also special ion-exchange resins, which, when necessary, can be used to bind up nitrate or phosphate, lowering levels of these pollutants quickly and effectively. Special filters filled with diatomaceous earth can be used to produce sparkling water and even reduce the number of micro-organisms in the water.

Guppies are extremely adaptable fishes that can live in the most varied types of water. But – and it this a big but – this applies mainly to guppies as a species, rather than to any specific individual.

But, because this is a practical rather than a philosophical treatise, in brief: as a rule you can keep and breed guppies successfully in whatever water comes out of your tap. At the same time, problems are more likely in soft than in hard water. Above all, guppies are exceptionally intolerant of pH swings, which, of course, occur more rapidly in soft water than in hard. If possible you should buy your guppies from a dealer nearby, as then there is a high probability that his water will have a similar composition to yours. If you have soft water, then I advise you most strongly to install an airstone in your aquarium. This will at least greatly reduce the likelihood of pH swings caused by carbon dioxide.

A guppy in robust good health. Optimal water conditions are the prerequisite of health.

The water in the guppy aquarium should always be clear and have a healthy smell. Guppies are intolerant of high populations of micro-organisms in the water and will rapidly react to this with shimmying body movements, clamped fins, and loss of appetite. In this case you must always immediately perform a large water change and eliminate the root cause. Too much food? Clogged filter? Clogged airstone? Always

check the nitrite level. Accelerated breathing and hanging/gasping at the surface are clear indications of nitrite toxicity.

Problems with adapting to your water will occur only with newly-acquired fishes, and the very first fry that they bring into the world will do well in your water without problems.

However, two special scenarios must be mentioned. If you have a domestic water softening unit in your house, the water from will be unsuitable for guppy maintenance. In such cases you must take the water for your aquarium from the mains, before it passes through the unit. If you have new copper pipework then the water from them will initially be suspect, as they need to develop a layer of oxide before the water is usable. Copper is highly poisonous to fishes.

Steer clear of salt in the guppy aquarium, as certain diseases may be triggered by it, even though guppies can live in pure sea water. More of this in the chapter on guppy diseases.

Guppies are naturally omnivorous, and can digest vegetable as well as animal food. As a rule a good quality flake food will form the basis of the aquarium diet and that suits guppies well. It is fair to say that any of the flake foods on the market is suitable. However, a number of serious errors are regularly made with flake food – by the aquarist, not the manufacturer. In order for the food to retain its nutritional value, care must be taken with its storage in the container. It must be kept cool, dry, and in the dark. Some of the ingredients of flake food, absolu-

This photo shows clearly the position, size, and form of the guppy mouth.

tely essential for fish nutrition, are easily spoiled – vitamins, unsaturated fatty acids, and other materials are adversely affected by oxygen, light, and moisture. Once the container has been opened the contents should be used within two weeks. Hence buying chea-

ply in bulk is a false economy! If you use an automatic feeder, it should be refilled with fresh food every day. Feed only as much as is eaten completely within five minutes. Guppies do not have large stomachs, and so should be fed three, better four, times per day.

In fact there is a difference between the sexes in this respect. Unlike females, male guppies can stuff their bellies full rapidly. This is dictated by their behavior – males spend much of their time in courtship, which uses energy on the one hand, and time on the other – so there is little time for feeding. Females, by contrast, spend the entire day feeding.

Guppies very much enjoy the highly nutritious sorts of frozen food. They are particularly fond of bloodworms, glassworms, and mosquito larvae, plus *Cyclops* and adult brine shrimps. One feed per day should be this type of food.

Worms such as Tubifex should be used sparingly, as they are rich in fats and hence unhealthy if fed too often. Tubifex must always be well-washed, as decaying worms can lead to poisoning if eaten.

Artemia nauplii (see the chapter on Hatching *Artemia*) are a special treat for guppies large and small, which cannot get enough of this food. When rearing fry, at least one feed per day should be with *Artemia* nauplii.

Like all life forms, guppies can suffer from a large variety of diseases. It is sensible to have available a number of medications, for the commonest fish diseases, so that treatment can be rapid in the event of infection.

The onset of disease is almost always evident from a striking change in behavior. If the guppy hangs list-lessly in a corner of the aquarium, swims with a noti-ceable wobbling motion, eats little, and clamps its fins, then these are warning signs. Often at this early stage of the disease it is still possi-ble to stimulate the natural immune response of the fish by performing a large water change and raising the normal maintenance temperature by 3-4 °C. Very many fish parasites die or are at least severely weakened if the temperature is somewhat higher than 30 °C. But note: at such high temperatures it is essential to observe the fish very closely. An airstone must always be placed in the aquarium when the temperature is raised to this degree. The oxygen-absorption capacity of water decrea-ses as temperature rises. Paradoxical-ly such high temperatures can also lead to oxygen toxicity through an excess of oxygen in the water if the aquarium is densely planted. At higher tempera-tures the plants will photosynthesize at a higher rate. An airstone will help in either eventuality.

During any period of treatment the temperature should not be allowed to drop at night. Because sick fishes eat very little, they should be fed only spa-ringly, if at all, in order to avoid additional harm to the patients through poor water quality. The most important method of treatment of fish diseases is prevention! This includes, of course, not just regular maintenance of the aquarium but also the quarantining of new arrivals. Never introduce a newly-purchased fish into an established fish population immediately. Every fish carries pathogens. This is not the fault of the breeder or dealer, it is simply the way things are.

This male guppy is seriously ill. The fins have been damaged by bacterial infection, and the fish is already severely emaciated.

Netting, transportation, and acclimatization to diffe-rent water conditions are all stressful, with negative effects on the fish. This can lead to an outbreak of disease that the fish would previously have fought off easily.

On the other hand, the fishes already swimming in your aquarium will also be carrying pathogens. The new arrival, in its weakened state, can very easily

The fin damage in this male guppy is not the result of disease, but mechanical injury. This is nothing to worry about, and will heal naturally.

Guppies are shoaling fishes and exhibit truly interesting behavior. It has already been mentioned, in the chapter Feeding guppies, that males and females have different feeding behavior. Males are busy practically the whole day courting females and competing among themselves, and hence spend relatively little time feeding, stuffing their bellies full when the opportunity arises.

Females, on the other hand, need to make provision for the next generation, and that means eat, eat, eat. Food is in short supply in the wild, and pregnancy is a difficult and energy-consuming time for females. Only well-nourished and healthy females stand a chance of withstanding

There is always something to watch with a shoal of guppies, and such an aquarium is never boring. These are feral guppies from Florida.

pathogens and evading predators. And the best way of ensuring the survival of the fry developing in their bellies is to take in as many calories as possible.

Females also grow appreciably larger than males, and therefore require more food right from the start in order to develop their body mass.

The courtship behavior is complex and interesting to watch. It begins with seeking behavior, in which the male actively searches for a female to court. Once he has found a potential partner, the first phase of

courtship begins, in which the male so to speak "introduces" himself. This involves his pursuing the female with his fins folded, swimming above, below, and next to her.

During this first phase of courtship a typical behavior is the touching of the posterior belly region with the mouth. The male then poses in front of the female, still with his fins folded against his body. All these actions serve to stimulate the female. If the female is suitably impressed by this display, she signals this by swimming slowly, and phase two can now begin. But

Guppy behavior

Courting guppy male during phase two of courtship.

ming towards the female at an angle from below with his gonopodium (copulatory organ) extended forward.

Guppies do not form a pair bond. They breed with anyone and everyone that they like and that is willing.

Interestingly, the basic elements of guppy courtship are inborn in every guppy, but are modified in the light of experience in the course of the fish's life. If you observe your guppies closely, then you will notice that there is both good and bad courtship. Some males give a textbook performance, while others try their hand at rape!

if she flees away, the whole performance starts again from scratch.

During phase two, the male seeks to adopt a head-to-head position with the female. Then he performs so-called courtship jumps, moving backwards away from the female, and then waits for her with fins folded. This phase of courtship allows the pair to synchronize, as the female must not make any sudden movement at the critical moment of the copulation itself. The courtship jumps are followed by the signal to copulate. Now the male displays in front of the female with his fins spread almost to splitting, and adopts an S-shaped body posture. The copulation itself lasts for only about a second, with the male swim-

Guppies are keen observers. They learn to adopt elements of courtship they have seen in other males. And there are tricksters and sneaks that lie in wait, watching the courtship of another male, and then charge in and mate with his female as soon as she responds, ousting the courting male and robbing him of the fruits of his labors.

Guppies are so human!

It is unwise to view animals as humans in a different form, as then it will be impossible to understand them. But there are nevertheless so many nice parallels between guppy and human behavior that we are often moved to smile.

Let us take the guppy female as an example. Young, inexperienced guppy females will respond to any show-off that courts them. Older, experienced females do not. Among guppies there are females that make the decision whether or not to mate. And only the most attractive males stand a chance with ripe ladies. Does this not ring a bell?

On the other hand, we have the male guppies. They spare no effort, dress themselves up, show off their strength, and all to win the favor of a female and increase their chances of distributing their sperm and thus their genes. But even if copulation takes place, a guppy male can never know if it was his sperm that resulted in guppy fry issuing from guppy eggs, as at each mating the females store up any unused sperm, which remains viable. Fresher sperm is preferred, though, and so males keep on striving to mate. Hope springs eternal......!

Among guppies, males, like females, respond to appearances. There are special black spots regarded as "sexy". In females there is the so-called gravid spot, which attracts males like magic (it has nothing to do with pregnancy, virgin females have it too). In males it is the black spots, contrasting dramatically with the orange elements of the coloration, that lead the females to make their choice. The more intense the spots and the more contrasting the coloration, the sexier the male in the eyes of the female. So much for "loving them for their minds".

I have already mentioned tricksters and mating sneaks. Guppies learn this through experience, as well. A male that repeatedly succeeds in mating without any great effort won't have just suddenly thought up this method of avoiding wasting time and energy on foreplay.

Perhaps it is observations of this kind that have turned so many people into enthusiastic aquarists. They make it clear that human problems – no matter how great – occur everywhere in nature and are really nothing special. This realization is very helpful in achieving a stress-free life.....

Here three males are competing for a female. Which one will she grant her favors?

The parts of a fish

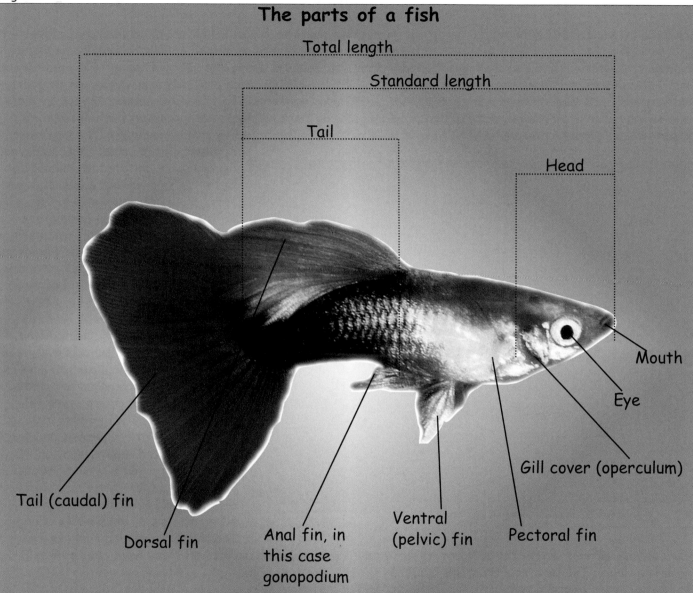

Total length

Standard length

Tail

Head

Mouth

Eye

Gill cover (operculum)

Tail (caudal) fin

Dorsal fin

Anal fin, in this case gonopodium

Ventral (pelvic) fin

Pectoral fin

Hatching *Artemia*

Artemia salina belongs to an ancient group of crustaceans, the so-called branchiopods (gill-feet). They are characterized by all species having adapted to periodic drying-up of their habitat by producing reproductive cysts, often termed eggs by aquarists. These "eggs" can survive in the bottom mud for weeks, months, even years of drought. Brine shrimps have adapted to a particularly saline habitat, although other branchiopods react rather badly to salt. Naturally, in their extreme habitat *Artemia* have no enemies and can proliferate massively – which is the basis of this small creature being used commercially as a fish food. The *Artemia* available in the trade originate mainly from the great salt lakes of the USA. Adult Artemia are about 1.5 cm long.

While most other food organisms live in waters also inhabited by fishes, this is not the case with *Artemia*. Hence brine shrimp are never carriers of fish diseases, *Artemia* is an indispensable food during the acclimatization of stress-sensitive wild-caught fishes.

Artemia eggs can be purchased at any aquarium store. Salt water is required for hatching, and the salt concentration should be between 3 and 8% (= 30-80 g/l). The simplest way is to add 3 rounded tablespoonsful of salt to a liter of water if nauplii are required quickly because unexpected breeding has taken place. Some nauplii will always hatch at this salinity. But for an optimal hatch rate, if time permits, it is necessary to experiment a little with the salinity. Very often the salinity required for an optimal hatch rate will vary somewhat from batch to batch of eggs. At a temperature of 18-32 °C the nauplii hatch after 24-36 hours. The hatching time is temperature dependent. The culture should be left to stand for 48 hours before harvesting to obtain the maximum "crop".

It is easiest to use ordinary household cooking salt for culturing *Artemia*. But you must always make sure that the cooking salt doesn't contain added fluorine or iodine salts, as the *Artemia* will not tolerate these. Cooking salt sometimes has additives to make it flow freely – these will not harm the *Artemia*, but they will affect the strength of the salt solution. Often by the end of the packet there is more flow agent than salt left. I therefore recommend coarse crystal cooking salt, as sold for salt mills. This contains no flow agents and is easy to measure . The use of salt intended for marine aquaria is a luxury, and this rather expensive salt does produce an exceptional hatch rate. It should above all be used if you want to rear the *Artemia* and feed them to larger fishes.

To hatch a large quantity of *Artemia* eggs (up to about half a tablespoonful) you will need an airpump, airline, and an empty 1 liter bottle (clear wine bottles have proved very good) or a manufactured *Artemia* hatchery. For continuous feeding it is best to use two bottles (cheers!) or two hatcheries. It is all very easy, except that some people may find the bubbling of the bottles and the humming of the airpump irritating. If only small amounts of brine shrimp are required (for about 30-50 fry) then there is no noise. In that case you need only small (300 ml) jam jars filled with salt solution, and a knife-tip-full of eggs sprinkled on the surface. The surface tension of the water will keep the eggs at the surface until they hatch, so they will have plenty of oxygen.

Artemia nauplii always swim towards the light (this behavior is termed positively photo-active). To harvest them, turn off the aeration and tilt the container slightly towards a strong light source. The nauplii will then congregate on the side nearest the light, while the most recently hatched, still very young, *Artemia* congregate at the bottom of the container. Now they can simply be siphoned off with airline into an *Artemia* sieve. Don't forget to turn the aeration back on!

Guppies in nature

Guppies can now be found anywhere in the world where the temperature never falls below 16 °C. There are few fish species that have so great a tolerance of a variety of water conditions as the guppy. In Indonesia I found them in drainage canals in the middle of towns. Anyone that enters these waters gets sick, but even so guppies live there. They were very colorful, but impossible to keep – as soon as they were placed in clean water they died.

Guppies have been introduced in many parts of the tropics to help combat dangerous mosquitos, whose larvae live in water where they are a favorite food of guppies. Whether or not guppies actually help control disease is uncertain. It was the observation that the large island of Barbados is fever-free that led to the guppy becoming a citizen of the world. The guppy is one of the very small number of freshwater fishes found on Barbados, so people concluded that logically it must be the Barbados guppy that kept the numbers of disease-bearing mosquitos down.

A wild guppy of unknown origin.

Back then (1910) there were sensible people who pointed out that there were also guppies in, for example, Trinidad and Venezuela, yet fever was rife there. Nevertheless it was decided to introduce guppies throughout the tropics. Then as now it was difficult to halt the bureaucratic process once started.

In places where well-meaning but ill-advised tropical doctors had not already done so, it was aquarists that introduced guppies. The worldwide trade in aquarium fishes allowed the guppy to travel to the ends of the Earth. Unfortunately many aquarists are irresponsible enough to release unwanted fishes into the wild, and this often has serious consequences for the native aquatic fauna. Thus the guppy became truly a citizen of the world. Even in Germany and Austria there are feral guppies in thermal springs.

In consequence it is now difficult to reconstruct the natural distribution of the guppy. It is quite certain that they have always inhabited northern South America, i.e. Venezuela and probably also the Guianas. The Lesser Antilles islands were colonized by guppies long ago, travelling via the sea route. How far Brazil is included in the natural range of the guppy is hard to say, but the possibility remains that the Amazon basin was colonized naturally by the species. There have always been natural barriers to its spread, along the coast in the form of low temperatures in southern South America, and on land the Andes. Either way, the Pacific drainages of South America are not part of the guppy's original range.

Trinidad has long served as a vast open-air laboratory for guppy research, and many of the facts about guppies cited here were first learned there. On Trinidad guppies prefer smaller streams that are largely plant-free. Every river, often even individual sections of rivers (e.g. those isolated by waterfalls that guppies cannot negotiate), has its own guppy population, distinct in both color and behavior.

Wild guppies like this are found near Rio de Janeiro in southern Brazil.

This wild guppy comes from the vicinity of Belém in Brazil, i.e. the lower Amazon.

A wild guppy from Peru, more precisely from the upper Amazon basin.

Piscivores as guppy breeders

The colorfulness of guppies in nature is determined above all by two factors: the females and the piscivores. While females prefer the most colorful of their suitors, these are also more likely to fall prey to piscivores.

In places where large piscivores lie in wait for guppies, the latter are least colorful. In places where small piscivores capture mainly guppy fry, the males can afford gaudier dress. But here too the piscivores control the breeding of the guppies, as in guppy populations with small piscivores sharing the habitat, the females mainly produce fewer and larger fry, while in populations confronted with larger piscivores, the females produce numerous but smaller offspring in each batch. On Trinidad the large piscivores are mainly cichlids of the genus *Crenicichla*, while the small piscivores are *Rivulus hartii*, a killifish species.

On Trinidad, *Rivulus hartii* produces guppy females with large fry.

Crenicichla (pike cichlids) produce pallid guppy males.

A wild guppy male from Venezuela. The pale coloration suggests that this fish comes from a water with a high predation pressure.

py. In places where fishes are the main predators, guppies flee instinctively towards the surface, and even jump out of the water, to escape their persecutors.

In places where the danger threatens largely from above the surface, guppies flee mainly towards the bottom, where they can hide among stones, roots, etc.

There are, of course, many intermediate stages between these two extremes, moreover guppies are able to learn. But even in line-bred guppies the two preferred flight patterns can be seen when they are frightened.

Guppies have many enemies. Not only fishes, but also large shrimps, insects, spiders, and fish-eating birds. This has an effect on the flight behavior of the gup-

If guppies are placed in, for example, a photographic aquarium, then some individuals will remain stubbornly at the surface, while others remain resting on the bottom.

These guppies have remained near the surface immediately after introduction to the photographic tank......

......and these near the bottom. Flight behavior is largely dictated genetically.

In guppy breeding, a distinction is made between base color and over-color. This is not just a case of what can be seen with the naked eye; rather the important point is that the base color is inherited independent of sex, while the genes for the over-color can be carried by either male or female.

The following are base colors:

Grey – the body is gray with darker scale edging (remember, the specific name of the guppy is reticulata (reticulated)).

The base color gray is genetically dominant over all other base colors.

Guppy female with base color blonde.

Whether or not a fish has dark scale edging is best seen on the back, as on the rest of the body the base color is often completely covered by the over-color.

Gold – likewise single-recessive. The color is like blonde, but the scales have a dark edging.

Blue – single-recessive, the body is blue.

Guppy female with base color gray.

Blonde – the commonest cultivated single-recessive base color. The body is light yellow, without dark scale edging.

Two guppy females with base color blue

Albino – a single recessive base color. Albinos are most easily recognized by their light red eyes.

Lutino – very similar to the albino, intense yellow body, dark red eyes. Single-recessive.

Lutino male. Note the dark red eyes. Because the over-color is very intense in males, the base color is easier to recognize in females.

Pink – a still problematical base color, probably single recessive. The body is yellow, the scales are dark-edged. The coloration resembles gold, but is lighter.

Female with base color pink. The base color gold is very similar.

The following base colors are double-recessive. Breeding them is difficult and low-yielding. In addition vitality is rapidly lost in double-recessive strains unless gray individuals are in-crossed from time to time. For these reasons the following colors are available only from specialist breeders, practically never in the trade.

White – the body is whitish, the color is a combination of base colors blonde and blue. These fishes sometimes look almost transparent and hence are an exquisite sight.

Cream – a combination of gold and blonde. Difficult to determine, but the light yellow body is somewhat darker than in blonde specimens.

Silver – this combination of gold and blue has a whitish-gray body with dark-edged scales.

Individuals with double-recessive base color are difficult to determine. So, is this a pale example of base color blue, or a fish with base color silver?

Finally, the base color albino-white is triple-recessive. These are snow-white individuals with bright red eyes. They are very difficult to breed and tricky to rear. For this reason they are rarely bred.

So much for the base colors. However, it is the so-called over-colors that make guppy males so colorful. As a rule they are inherited via the males. A well-known and important exception is the gene that causes the posterior half of the body to be black ("half-black"), which can be inherited by males and females.

So, what is the difference between base color and over-color in practice? Quite simply, if I want to breed a guppy with a particular coloration, then first of all I need a pure strain of the desired base color, because only thus can the results of a cross be cros-sed further such that the end product is the fish desired.

An example: I have a particularly beautiful male of the snakeskin type, whose base color is gray. But I want to breed only snakeskin guppies with the base color blonde. So, I mate my fine male with a blonde female. If there are now blonde specimens in the first batch from this mating, then the snakeskin male carries genes for both base colors, and our goal is already achieved. Now all I need do is to mate the blonde siblings of this first generation and the result will always be blonde snakeskin. But it may happen that there is not a single blonde among the offspring of the original mating, in which case the original male is pure-strain gray, and this color is dominant over blonde. However, all his sons are now mixed-strain.

The finest son can now be crossed with another blonde female or one of his sisters to produce a few offspring with the desired pattern – blonde snakeskin. Mating these siblings with one another will lead to the desired strain.

Of course, "there's many a slip twixt cup and lip", and "Murphy's Law" often plays a role here as elsewhere. The snakeskin factor is carried only by males. It is incredible how in individual cases the statistical ratio of the sexes in guppy broods (about 50% males and 50% females come into the world) can suddenly undergo a shift, so that, for example, all the blonde young are females. Or there may be a few males, but they totally

Two attractive snakeskin males with base color gray. The international trade calls this form King Cobra.

Guppy breeding in practice

The mating of gray snakeskin with blonde female........

matings are then needed to eliminate genetic factors at the halfway stage. And time is limited, as our original "dream male" will not live forever. It is, however, necessary to mate him with his daughters in order to fix the desired characteristics. For this we need to know the genetic make-up of the daughters. For this it is essential that the breeding females are kept virgin, to prevent the risk of stored sperm from some other male being responsible for fertilization.

In practice therefore the father will be mated with as many of his daughters as possible. These must be kept isolated singly, so that we can be quite sure which young come from which mother. If the males lack the splendor of their father.

Be that as it may, the above was a rather simple example. It is generally relatively easy to breed new over-colors from gray onto single-recessive base colors, as the individuals that exhibit the recessive base color are always pure-strain. By contrast it is far harder when breeding with the base color gray, as all sorts of genetic permutations may result (more of this on blue pages 48&49). Because it is impossible to tell whether the male is pure- or mixed-strain, it is more than wise to resort to females of a pure strain for mating. Even so it remains complicated enough, as if the male is mixed-strain then only a quarter of the offspring will be pure-strain gray. Extensive sibling

.........produces a relatively blonde snakeskin – easy if you know how!

in a brood are uniform in appearance then there is also a high probability that the females will breed true. Now sibling matings can be undertaken to try and fix the strain.

However, we should also carry out parallel, sibling matings among the first (F1) generation, to have an ace up our sleeves in case the father-daughter matings fail to produce the desired result.

This not only sounds complicated – it is! Without a carefully-maintained record book, in which all matings – and, above all, their results - are painstakingly entered, it is impossible ever to achieve a pure strain. Much knowledge, breeding skill, and scientifically-precise work are prerequisites of success. It is thus easy to see why, when a new guppy variety arrives on the market, often after years of work, the proud breeder gives it a fine-sounding name. A few of these are mentioned in this book.

At the same time the commercial breeders in Asia, Israel, and the USA have different problems to contend with than do hobby breeders worldwide. In the hobby the individual fish is far more pivotal, the number of fish involved is far smaller. A commercial breeder must be able to supply thousands on a regular basis, and these fishes must be not only beautiful but also in A1 health, as they face days or weeks of stress before they eventually find homes in private aquaria.

Here we see a snakeskin male with base color blonde and over-color red.

This male also has base color blonde and over-color red.

Guppy breeding in practice

A blonde half-black male with red over-color.

This is what the same combination (half-black/over-color red) looks like in a fish with base color gray.

Guppy breeding in practice

A blonde female with the half-black gene. Over-colors are hard to determine in females. This one has the over-colors multicoloured.

Can you guess what this male is termed?

(base color gray, over-color multicolored)

Father Mendel counts his peas

Until the 20th century the breeding of domesticated animals and plants was largely a matter of trial and error. In fact the monk Gregor Mendel had already discovered, back in 1864, that inheritance follows rules that can be expressed statistically. But, as so often in the case of genius, his work was not appreciated during his lifetime, and it was not until 1900 that the immense significance of his discoveries was recognized. Nowadays genetics is an extremely complex branch of science ("gene technology" and "cloning" are now everyday terms), but Mendel's basic laws are adequate for fish breeding.

In the monastery garden Mendel had four sorts of peas. In one type the peas were green and round, in the second yellow and round, in the third green and wrinkled, and in the fourth yellow and wrinkled. The brilliant thing about the choice of peas is that they can be counted, and mathematical rules be deduced regarding inheritance. So, Mendel grew peas, and Mendel counted peas, and he discovered:

Mendel's first law, the law of uniformity.

This states that if two pure-strain forms are crossed, the offspring will all look the same. At the same time he discovered that characteristics may be dominant or recessive (potentially suppressed). If two equivalent forms are crossed (i.e. dominant x dominant or recessive x recessive) then the offspring will be intermediate to the parents in appearance. If, on the other hand, dominant is crossed with recessive, then the F1 (first generation) offspring will look like the dominant form.

Mendel quickly realized that there was a difference between appearance and inherited characteristics, and so he distinguished between the genotype (inherited characteristics) and the phenotype (external appearance).
If the F1 offspring of across are crossed with one another,

then we get

Mendel's second law, the law of divergence.

For now the F2 offspring diverge from the uniform phenotype in accordance with their genotypes. If the forms in the original parent stock (the P generation) were equivalent, then the F2 will comprise exactly one quarter offspring that look like one parent, one quarter that look like the other parent, and two quarters that look like the F1. If the F1 derives from a dominant-recessive cross, then three quarters of the F2 will look like the dominant parent, but only one quarter will be pure-strain, and the other two quarters mixed-strain. The remaining quarter of the F2 will look like the recessive parent and be pure-strain. The ratio of the mix of genotypes in the F2 is always 1:2:1, regardless of the cross from which the F1 originated.

All this applies as long as we are looking at a single phenotypic character – in peas, for example, color (green or yellow) or texture (smooth or wrinkled). But what happens if we consider both characters simultaneously? Mendel crossed and counted and discovered

Mendel's third law, the recombination of genes.

Each phenotypic character is inherited independently in accordance with Mendel's first two laws. If two forms are crossed that differ in both characters (green + smooth x yellow + wrinkled) then the phenotypic characters green and yellow are inherited according to the first law, and smooth and wrinkled likewise. If green is dominant, yellow recessive, smooth dominant, and wrinkled recessive, then the F1 will contain only smooth green peas, while the F2 will have 9 parts green + smooth, 3 parts green + wrinkled, 3 parts yellow and smooth, and 1 part yellow and wrinkled.

Mendel and fish-breeding

Mendel's first law, experiment 1. Red and blue are dominant colors.

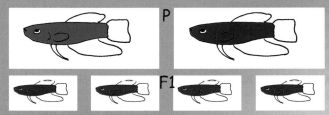

Mendel's first law, experiment 2. Red is dominant, blue recessive.

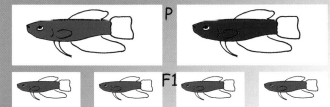

Mendel's second law, experiment 3. Crossing two individuals from the dominant/dominant cross (experiment 1).

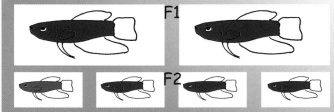

Mendel's second law, experiment 4. Crossing two individuals from the dominant/recessive cross (experiment 2).

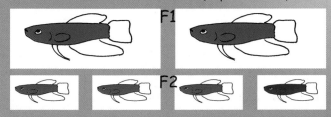

Mendel's third law, experiment 5. Red is dominant, blue recessive, round-tail dominant, scissor-tail recessive.

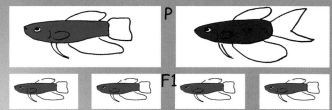

Mendel's third law, experiment 6. Crossing two F1 individuals from experiment 5.

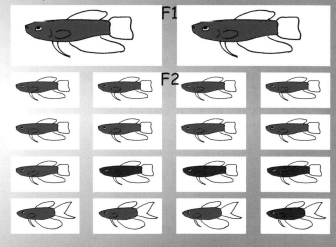

Alleles (the term for the pairs of genes responsible for a phenotypic character) are best expressed using letters. Dominant alleles are written as upper case letters, recessives as lower case. Thus experiments 1 and 3 can be written as follows:

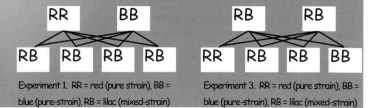

Experiment 1. RR = red (pure strain), BB = blue (pure-strain), RB = lilac (mixed-strain)

Experiment 3. RR = red (pure strain), BB = blue (pure-strain), RB = lilac (mixed-strain)

Tail forms

The scissor-tail is very similar to the double-sword, but the center of the caudal fin is very deeply indented. I personally have never seen this form; it is no longer mentioned in recent books and may have died out.

In the lyre tail the ends of both swords are turned outwards.

Long-tail types

The flag-tail, in which the upper and lower edges of the fin are straight, is rarely bred nowadays.

The veil-tail is a very harmonious form. The upper and lower edges of the fin run in a gentle curve.

The fan-tail is a very popular form. The tail is triangular

and ideally its upper and lower edges should form an angle of 45 ° with the body.

The delta-tail is currently the most popular cultivated form. Very similar to the fan-tail, but in this case the upper and lower edges form an angle of 70 ° to the body axis.

As well as these standard forms there are also the so-called Giessen and Berlin guppies, in which all the fins are elongated. The Berlin guppy may have died out, its capacity for life was very limited. The Giessen guppy, on the other hand, is still bred, at least in Asia, as the "ribbon guppy". The genes for fin elongation are dominant. These fishes are best bred not as pure strains, but regularly crossed with other strains.

Not only males, but also females, have an influence on the tail form of their sons. Instead of making life difficult, it is best, when starting to create a new strain, to use females appropriate to the desired objective!

Round-tail females look like wild guppy females, sword-tail females are rather elongate, and large-tail females, like their male counterparts, have much enlarged tails.

The dorsal fin can be enlarged, but this is not necessary. This applies to males and females of all types.

A lutino Giessen guppy, photographed at an exhibition in Japan.

The various fin forms are already present in the wild guppy.   This a wild male with a top-sword.

Breeding livestock brings responsibilities. Even though all the changes that can be bred into guppies have already been programmed by Mother Nature, that does not mean that we should abuse here bounty.

The object of line-breeding should always be to produce happy healthy guppies. This relates particularly to fin size. Guppy males with excessively large tails are seriously limited in their swimming ability. Often they can no longer perform the courtship ritual properly. In addition, in the course of the fish's life its spine may become curved due to the weight of the tail, restricting its movement still further.

It is up to the breeder to police his own activities. It is, of course, difficult to say whether the guppy with an outsize tail suffers pain, but it is certainly condemned to a life sentence. In fact such fishes probably don't suffer, as they exhibit no behavioral abnormalities that might reflect pain. But the activity levels of such fishes are nevertheless seriously limited, and hence it is important, when breeding large-tail types, to make sure that an otherwise top-quality male does not exhibit the symptoms described above.

The days when all guppy females were "ugly ducklings" are long past. During the breeding of fancy guppies with large tails, females have also acquired fine feathers.

Half-black gray delta-tail with a very large tail.

This colorful delta-tail is very well developed and harmonious.

High-bred fancy guppies

The tail of this lutino male is far too large for European tastes. The fish can only with difficulty maintain a slanting body position.

High-bred fancy guppies are generally sought in vain in the aquarium trade, where the majority of guppies originate from professional breeders who place less value on fin standards (large-tails are mostly bred) than on markings that are as uniform as possible. Moreover, high-bred guppies are very expensive. The

However, as a rule breeders keep all their females for further breeding, so if any high-bred fish are available at all, they are generally males. But it is still a huge saving on effort, to have fixed-strain males with which to start a breeding program.

There are guppy societies all over the world that also stage shows. These are worth visiting if you are interested in unusual guppies. You will find addresses and links on our home page, www.aqualog.de.

Guppies from professional breeders are usually very pretty, but their finnage is rarely up to scratch.

reasons for this should be clear. Nonetheless it may happen that a breeder stops breeding a strain and then his broodstock may appear in the trade at a relatively cheap price. This way pure-strain fishes can be obtained quickly and easily.

One of the most popular guppies from commercial breeders is the "King Cobra", a yellow snakeskin/filigree guppy with base color gray.

This round-tail guppy was christened "Rio Negro" by its breeder.

A double-sword guppy from a commercial breeder in Asia.

Guppy picture gallery

A so-called "Moscow guppy". In this fish the anterior body is very dark. By crossing this type with half-blacks it is possible to produce almost completely black guppies.

A guppy with metallic over-color, named "Eldorado" by the breeders.

Guppy picture gallery

This cultivated form, called "Neon Blue", is currently one of the most popular guppies.

Scientifically speaking, guppies belong to the genus *Poecilia*. Various subgenera are recognized within this genus, and many scientists regard these as separate genera. Guppies belong to the subgenus *Acanthocephalus*.

At present this subgenus contains only one scientifically described species – our guppy. A second species, Endler's guppy, is at present being scientifically studied but as yet has no species name. Hence it should for the time being be referred to scientifically as *Poecilia (Acanthocephalus)* sp. (sp. stands for species).

This small, very beautiful livebearer was collected in Venezuela in 1975 by the guppy researcher John END-LER, in the Laguna de Patos, Cumana, in the north-east of the country. The warm (27 °C) water was dark green with unicellular algae. Endler is a behavioralist, not a systematist, so he passed specimens to the leading systematist for livebearing toothcarps, Donn ROSEN, for study, but Rosen died before he could name the species. However, he had given a few specimens to Klaus KALLMANN, who brought them to Germany as Endler's guppy, and from Germany these attractive fishes were distributed across Europe, Japan, and the USA. Endler himself didn't know about this until 1980, when he received enquiries about the fish. Unfortunately it seems that Endler's guppy has been crossed with normal guppies (which also occur in the Laguna de Patos), so that pure-blooded specimens are rarely found. Distinguishing characters are, for example, a large black lateral spot in the form of an elongate "S" lying on its side, a golden stripe, beginning behind the eye and running about a third of the length of the body, and the fact that some males (about 20% in the wild) have black pectoral fins. In wild guppies these fins are always transparent.

Endler's guppy is not an isolated population of the guppy, as the latter also occurs in the Laguna de Patos, although it prefers the affluent streams with somewhat cooler (25°C) and clear water, and is rarely to be found in the laguna itself.

Sadly this species is seriously endangered, perhaps already extinct, in the wild, as industrial waste-water is discharged into the Laguna de Patos. So far no other locations are known for the species. Anyone who is able to obtain any of these fishes should always breed them true, and never cross them with ordinary guppies! They are not difficult to keep and breed, but are short-lived (only about a year).

A pure-blooded Endler's guppy.

The wild relatives of the guppy

The six species of the genus *Micropoecilia* are closely related to the guppies, and sometimes confused with them. Unfortunately, unlike guppies, they are real problem fishes, whose maintenance and breeding present immense difficulties even for experienced aquarists. They are thus only very rarely seen in the trade, and then at high prices, even though they are very common in the wild.

Micropoecilia branneri, Branner´s livebearer

Micropoecilia amazonica, Amazon livebearer

Micropoecilia parae, Variable mini

Micropoecilia bifurca, Small amazon livebearer

Micropoecilia picta, Black banded mini

This new cultivated form is called "Micarif".

"Multi Cobra" - available for somewhat longer, but very popular.

Eclipse™ Aquarium System

ADVANCED TECHNOLOGY, SUPERIOR PERFORMANCE, UNLIMITED VERSATILITY...

Superior BIO-Wheel Filtration
Silent, high capacity 3-stage efficiency. BIO-Wheel and Eclipse Filter Cartridge unmatched by all other types of aquarium filtration.

Superior Illumination
Colour-enhancing fluorescent lighting. Far better that heat-producing incandescent bulbs. Plants thrive and colours of fish and plants come alive!

Superior Convenience
Easy set-up, easy operation. Polymer wool and carbon all-in-one filter cartridge changes in seconds, whilst the BIO-Wheel never needs replacing.

Superior View
Injection-molded acrylic aquarium provides a panoramic 360 degrees of prime viewing area for maximum enjoyment. Available as *Eclipse System 3* and *Eclipse Systems 6*.

Eclipse Explorer
Employs the same sophisticated BIO-Wheel filtration technology as the larger Eclipse Systems. Available in 4 additional fun colours, incorporating a textured skylight to maximise surrounding light.

Explorer = 7.5 litres System 3 = 11 litres Sytem6 = 22.5 litres

ALL AQUALOG TITLES & THE ABOVE PRODUCTS ARE DISTRIBUTED IN THE UK BY:

Specialists in Aquarium & Pet Technology

Belton Road West ~ Loughborough
Leicestershire ~ LE11 5TR
Tel: 01509 610310 ~ Fax: 01509 610304
E-mail: info@underworldproducts.co.uk
Web Site: www.underworldproducts.co.uk

All the important information at a glance:

- **Color photos of all the fishes of a group (inc. all varieties, color and cultivated forms)**
- **Identification of any fish is accurate and easy: scientific name, hobby name, Aqualog code number**
- **Easy-to-understand text, international maintenance symbols**
- **Newly discovered fishes published as supplements: your lexicon will always remain up-to-date!**

All rainbows
(H. Hieronimus)

All the colors of the rainbow, as the name implies. All species known to date are to be found in this book, but many more remain to be discovered in biotopes, eg in Papua New Guinea, where collecting is extremely difficult.

(144 pages, 700 approx. color photos)
ISBN 3-931702-80-4
Item no. B013

All livebearers
(M. Kempkes, F. Schäfer)

For the first time all the livebearers are illustrated – the well-known guppy, mollies, swordtails, platies, plus all the others. All the wild and cultivated forms/color varieties, as well as the halfbeaks.

(352 pages, 2000 approx. color photos)
ISBN 3-931702-77-4
Item no. B009

All Corydoras
(U. Glaser sen.)

All the mailed catfishes are presented together for the first time. As well as the genera Aspidoras, Brochis, Callichthys, Corydoras, Dianema, and Hoplosternum, there are also all variants, mutants, hybrids, cultivated forms, and undescribed species ("C-No").

(144 pages, 650 color photos)
ISBN 3-931702-13-8
Item no. B004

LORICARIIDAE – All L-Numbers
(U. Glaser sen.)

All L-number catfishes up to L204, with the rest as supplements. The only book to illustrate and describe all the L-number catfishes.

(112 pages, 450 approx. color photos)
ISBN 3-931702-01-4
Item no. B001

**African Cichlids I
MALAWI MBUNA**
(E. Schraml)

This book really does show mbuna species and varia covered in the lake to dat

(240 pages, 1500 approx photos)
ISBN 3-931702-79-0
Item no. B012

All Goldfish and Varieties
(K. H. Bernhardt)

The goldfish is the oldest ornamental fish in the world, familiar to everyone - but how many people know that there are so incredibly many varieties? This pictorial lexicon includes all the forms and color variants.

(160 pages, 690 color photos)
ISBN 3-931702-78-2
Item no. B011

All Labyrinths
(F. Schäfer)

For the first time a compact lexicon illustrating all the labyrinth fishes. Plus the snakeheads, nandids, Pristolepidae and Badidae which exhibit many behavioral parallels with the labyrinths. Also includes an identification key to the genus Betta. The official reference guide for labyrinthfish societies worldwide as soon as it was published.

(144 pages, 690 color photos)
ISBN 3-931702-21-9
Item no. B006

Book + CD-ROM

All books incl. CD-ROM

- **This series of books portrays fishes of various groups using top-quality color photos**
- **Unambiguous identification via international code numbers, scientific and hobby names**
- **Brief details: Characteristics, maintenance requirements, etc.**
- **All photos in each book also on the accompanying CD-ROM**

Version A: German, Japanese, Czech, Turkish, Hungarian
Version B: English, Dutch, Swedish, Danish, Finnish
Version C: French, Spanish, Italian, Polish, Mandarin

Photo collection No. 1
(U. Glaser sen.)
African catfishes
A: ISBN 3-931702-56-1
B: ISBN 3-931702-57-X
C: ISBN 3-931702-58-8
Item no. PC001-A/B/C

Photo collection No. 2
(U. Glaser sen.)
Characins 1
(African characins, predatory characins, pencilfishes)
A: ISBN 3-931702-59-6
B: ISBN 3-931702-62-6
C: ISBN 3-931702-63-4
Item no. PC002-A/B/C

Photo collection No. 3
(U. Glaser sen.)
Characins 2
(Piranhas, silver dollars, headstanders, hatchetfishes)
A: ISBN 3-931702-64-2
B: ISBN 3-931702-65-0
C: ISBN 3-931702-66-9
Item no. PC003-A/B/C

Photo collection No. 4
(U. Glaser sen.)
Characins 3
(Neons, Moenkhausia, A can predatory characins, characins)
A: ISBN 3-931702-81-2
B: ISBN 3-931702-44-8
C: ISBN 3-931702-47-2
Item no. PC004-A/B/C

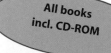

Each volume contains 96-112 pages and approx. 300-400 color photos